Anne Tardos

UXUDO

TUUMBA PRESS / Berkeley
O BOOKS / Oakland

with the participation of ghos-ti

The author wishes to thank the editors of *Conjunctions* #30 for publishing
Toowomba 1, Toowomba 2, Toowomba 5, WorkAnts, Summerdrum, and Who Knew?
The editors of *Chain* #5 for publishing Berthe, Monkey Ghost, Efnogla 2, Efnogla 3,
Hochgeduld, Mozart, Uxudo, Fudd-razz, Con-Lon 1, and Con-Lon 2.
The editors of *The Germ* #2 for publishing Escargots, Efnogla 1, and Let's Try This 2.
The editors of *Canticsyst,* for publishing Dee Eye-Luh, She Put It Mildly, and Hil de Gard.
And the editors of *Trembling Ladders* (Australia) for publishing earlier versions.

ISBN 1-891190-99-7
FIRST PRINTING

Library of Congress Catalog Card Number: 99-95113
Library of Congress Cataloging-in-Publication Data
1. Tardos, Anne, 1943-
2. Multilingualism
3. Imaginary languages
4. Visual poetry

Typesetting, book and cover design by Anne Tardos
Printed in the United States of America, by Thomson-Shore, Inc.

TUUMBA PRESS / BERKELEY
O BOOKS / OAKLAND

Tuumba Press and O Books are distributed by Small Press Distribution
1341 Seventh Street Berkeley, CA 94710

FOREWORD BY CAROLINE BERGVALL

It is in the rapid language switches that the plurilingual text first and foremost announces itself. It's in the stop-start structure which roots out the languages framed and in use, and the various ways in which they intersect, through mixed speech, borrowings and compounds, and neologistic sounding games, that the mechanics and polemics of such a textual environment find themselves defined. The reader, pressed hard between words written in language they don't know, words written in language they know, words written in language they thought they knew.

Issues of stylistic opaqueness brush against the live question of cultural idioms and language differences. The fraught nature of translatability is played out across numerous stylised and untranslatable translation games. Is what I cannot comprehend another language, a trick of the text, the slip of a tongue. Translatability (problematising it) becomes a vital aspect of the structure. A regulator as much as a modulator. The phonetic spelling out of sounds and sound associations, for instance, guides the reader across pronunciation borders. It seems to act as a geling factor, yet successfully fails to standardise the languages of the text. Nonsensical, sonic play on and of words is here more than a stylistic banter. Closer to a linguistic dissonance which would wear the ironies of its whereabouts on the narrows of a sleeve.

Similarly, words, nouns, familiar expressions, echoes of conversation, shrapnels of speech, or song, are explored, teased out, seem to organise themselves into parallel cumulative structures, dispute the legitimacies of syntactical ordering to show up the synchronic displays of multiple languages.

The intricacies of such disruptive, uprooted dealings inevitably add humourous correspondences to the work. Nothing equals another thing equals another equals another. In cross-lingual pollination, the linguistic sign seems as differential as any saussurean stylistics might wish for it. And the sonic games, cross-lingual puns, private riddles and neological turns which, rather gleefully, punctuate most of the plurilingual work I have come across, would seem to push this point.

Yet each node, pivot, moment of switch from one language to another jolts and ties differentiality to the thorny question of cultural origination and linguistic diversity. As a textual mode or genre, plurilingual writing is openly predicated on the structuring of particularised cultural exchanges and on playing out the linguistic flexibilities of polyglots and cultural migrants. Indeed, the link between literary strategy and cultural belonging, between language acquisition and textual disposition, between the private and the public, the emotive, mundane and the artifactual, aestheticised experience of cultural idioms, is by definition at the heart of such textuality and provides the text with its conceptual as well as more personal motifs.

The plurilingual text saturates language with languages. It develops strategies out of the detailed perception and experience of borders: borderlines: boundaries: where are they: what are they: do they do: to the tongue: to the body: to the organisation of memory: in the sentence: in the understanding of what is and what is not: translatable. It plays the histories and coded treacheries of monolingual alliances at their own game, yet does not respond to the modern locus of origin and exile and sublimation. Critically, it takes on board the idea of belonging as a task, a piecemeal, contextualising affair.

Indeed, cultural allegiance is not experienced as necessarily predicated on linguistic origin. And the sense of linguistic belonging is in turn neither necessarily nor clearly predicated on the acquisition of one's "first" language. In fact, the very notion of a first language is up for grabs. Shall we call "first" the one(s) you were brought into or the one(s) you use daily or the one(s) you are asked to read the text in. Of these, which one would be "the" one.

Thinking about the accent Conrad never lost, is "the" one located in the mouth. Is it located in the glottis. Is this where mother lodges the tongue.

My linguistic body walks in the split fields of experience that each tongue brings in. I have many tongues does this give me many mothers. She has rooted her own language in my languages yet mother is neither tongue nor country. I cannot return to and I don't. No return where there was always more than one departure. Instead, I turn to and that is where I find her.

It is often argued that bilingualism itself ought to be considered a first language. Would this, could this, include silence. That which takes the place of language acquisition when excised by political or cultural impositions. That which knows that questions of ancestry and access to familial antecedents find themselves more often than not tied up with the experience of uprootedness and lack of access. And that to return is full of mournful contradictions and impossible retrievals which are mixed in with the twists and turns of chosen or enforced linguistic affiliations. Nothing equals absolutely. Everything indelible is relational.

Cultural fixation on origin and the naturalisation of etymological and social filiations is fundamentally refuted by a textuality which disturbs the hegemony of monolingualism. Intimately, inherently it throws up the xenophobic asymmetries of difference (which one's good which one's not which one's to keep which one's to throw out).

Perhaps for this reason, does the act of remembering, as a turning to, rather than a returning, that is, as one which enables a constitutive activity of memory, play such a vital part in setting up the grounds for writing. Samples, physical "proofs" of displacement, of relocation, of having-been "there" and "here", are, elliptically or outright, gathered up from (auto)biographical, familial material, scavenged through for personal (personalised) use. Some of which verbal, some visual.

What proofing of the video or photo-album takes place that verbal language might not retain, works alongside the multiplicity of speech and the subliminal logic of sounds: emotive jolts: physiological graphs: recorded takes of diagonal lines. The writer will treat the image as she treats nominative chains. Loosely, fluidly, ludically, the text-image compounds are worked to form an inseparable tracking down of the physiologies of memory.

This framed echo-chamber does not illustrate nor translate. Nor does it erase its elements into one, seamless, cohesive readerliness. It enriches its gymnastics of clues and games of tones with clashes between personal grammars and social usage. Only the precision of such divided attentions can carry off the emotive and psycho-social genealogies which the plurilingual text is interjecting into the overall cultural body.

London, 1999

Contents

Foreword by Caroline Bergvall	7
Author's Preface and Acknowledgments	13
"All sins of all cats rolled into one"	18-19
"Da saßen sie also"	20-21
Affengespenst	22-23
Efnogla - 1	24-25
Efnogla - 2	26-27
Efnogla - 3	28-29
"Hochgeduld after nine from a fountain"	30-31
"Steigen Sie in den Tram?"	32-33
"Hast du's vielleicht vergessen wollen?"	34-35
ArbeitsAmeisen	36-37
A Seat, a Stretch, a Rivertwist	38-39
Escargots	40-41
"Lorraine hug-a-bee hiába"	42-43
Who knew?	44-45
Love	46-47
Bild	48-49
Painting	50-51
"Szép anyag didn't run Summerdrum"	52-53
She Put It Mildly	54-55
Toowomba 1	56-57
Toowomba 2	58-59
Toowomba 3	60-61
Toowomba 4	62-63
Toowomba 5	64-65
Toowomba 6	66-67
Toowomba 7	68-69
Toowomba 8	70-71
Hil de Gard	72-73
Let's Try This - 1	74-75
Let's Try This - 2	76-77
Furfangos - 1	78-79
Furfangos - 2	80-81
For DGR and the PRB	82-83
"Fodrász pink apricot"	84-85
Con-Lon - 1 & Con-Lon - 2	86-87
"Looking forward into"	88-89
Dee Eye-luh	90-91

AUTHOR'S PREFACE & ACKNOWLEDGMENTS

Uxudo is a series of two-page works. I wrote poems in several languages, usually English, French, German, and Hungarian, along with neologisms and other linguistic inventions.

I selected individual video frames, which I modified and edited using a number of graphics programs. Then I assembled these images with the poems. Once the two elements were together, I often edited the poems because the nature of the page had changed.

All the images featured in this book (except for the clip-art dog on page 74) were captured from a single videotape I made of my friends and family in Vienna in June 1997, after the death of my mother. I wrote all the poems around the same time.

The left-hand pages serve as a kind of legend to the right-hand pages, providing some translations, transliterations, and other clarifications. Invented words are either left unexplained or else are indicated by a repeating equals sign, as in

"glupf = glupf = glupf" or "uxudo = uxudo = uxudo."

Translatable words and phrases are treated as

"quake = tremblement = Beben = rengés"

or as "*Mitgefühl* [mitt-gu-fuel] = compassion."

Phonetic transcriptions are often placed inside square brackets and are almost always geared to the English reader. Sometimes I address the German, French, or Hungarian speaker, and provide transliterations and translations on the left-hand pages as I think necessary, almost never identifying a language, since I assume that readers will be able to pick out the ones in their own language. Over time, these left-hand pages became an integral part of the texts and are now, of course, poems in their own right.

I found the word "uxudo" on a page of output errors of my printer. It could have been a random occurrence of letters appearing next to each other, or maybe it is part of an intramachine command not meant for human eyes. I have a collection of such monoprints, mostly of graphics, that printed out only once in a very special way and that I could never reproduce. "Uxudo," then, is a gift from the technology I use.

Recently I was asked by a friend, who is also fluent in French and English, whether my texts tell stories or recount experiences. I couldn't answer with a simple "no," although I would have liked to. I told her that in these poems I did not, at least not consciously, try to describe anything. They were written by letting one word lead me to another, by way of some sort of association. In psychiatry, this level of consciousness is referred to as liminal.

This writing is often a kind of musical composition using language. Neologisms like "multiplicatering" or "gewurzeltidé" are a kind of play with established words, while

13

others, such as "shano-glick" or "gelinkami," are not obvious derivations of existing words and exist more for their pure sound than for any contextual association.

When I felt that the reader could use my help, as with the Hungarian word "fodrász" [FUDD-razz] = hairdresser, I offered it. Such a word has a "story" of its own and is laden with associations.

Other parts of the poems, such as "Ivan was terrible" are simple statements. Poems like these, written by going from one image or word to another and not by knowingly telling a story, might later reveal, often surprisingly clear, scenarios. So the process is not that of remembering and putting into words a particular event, but rather of writing something (maybe unexplainable) that is happening at the moment of writing. It would follow that the reading of such a poem could become a similar process of discovering underlying concerns and motivations. So, in fact, my friend was not far from the truth when she said that I was no doubt describing an experience.

Why all these languages and why mix them? I should begin by explaining that I was born in France and, at the age of five, moved to Hungary with my Hungarian father and Austrian mother, who spoke French with one another, because neither spoke the other's native language. French was also the only language I knew at the time. Thus we all continued speaking French while living in Budapest. I learned Hungarian as quickly as any five-year-old would, although I remember the struggles against incomprehension even then. Complicating things even more, my parents elected to send me to the Russian-language school of Budapest, the Gorki School, where the Russian ruling class's children went. The Russian children did not learn any Hungarian, I remember, but I had to learn Russian in order to keep up. I have forgotten most of that language.

In early 1957, at the age of twelve, I was sent to live in Vienna, because Budapest had become a dangerous and unstable place, where writers and other intellectuals were imprisoned and executed. My father was a writer and was imprisoned there for over two years. (Today he lives in Paris and is a chevalier of the Legion of Honor.) In Vienna I learned to speak German while going to a French lycée. German, the language spoken by Austrians, was then my third—or if you count Russian—my fourth language. (But let's not count it, because I've forgotten so much of it.) French was the only language besides Hungarian that I knew at the time. This was not a smooth transition, as the language and cultural background of my education between ages five and twelve was not French, but Russian and Hungarian. I was at sea in the lycée when it came to the Crusades or even Molière.

In 1964, after a visit to New York, I decided to move here permanently. I was more comfortable in a culture which was largely made up of people from elsewhere. A society in which cultural, linguistic, and even racial mixing was at least conceivable seemed to me the most natural. Today, some thirty years later, this form of internationalism and cosmopolitanism makes more sense than ever for a complex society.

14

Geographical displacement was not new to me. Even as a little child I remember moving from place to place. I was born during the Second World War, and my parents, who were freedom fighters in the French Resistance, were always on the run from the Nazis. Once they had me, they became even easier targets than before, and later they told me of wigs and disguises they had worn and how they once fled from their little house in Cannes in the middle of the night and, looking back, saw the Gestapo shooting into their house, assuming they were hiding in the closet, as people often did in those days. Lights being turned on in the night and hasty packing of bags are among my earliest memories.

It is safe to say, then, that I achieved a certain universality in my travels and that ignoring the continual presence of the four languages I know nearly equally well, as well as ignoring my years of work in the visual arts, would be denying myself a richness I've earned. So I write these multi-, poly-, plurilingual poems and carefully combine them with my images to make these artworks.

The publishers of this book, Lyn Hejinian (Tuumba Press) and Leslie Scalapino (O Books), have given me their unfailing friendship and support. Their graciousness and generosity made this publication possible and my gratitude to them is enormous.

I wish to thank Travis Ortiz, co-editor of Atelos and publisher of ghos-ti, for his enthusiasm and support. Without his help I would not have explored the Adobe PageMaker typesetting program as thoroughly as I did. I originally composed these pages using that program because I needed the flexibility of combining and moving texts and images freely on the page. Putting the elements together to make up a book turned out to be an unexpected and challenging experience. Thanks to Laurie Briegel, of Thomson-Shore, for her calm and intelligent guidance during the typesetting. Deborah Thomas, publisher of *Extra!*, the magazine of Fairness & Accuracy In Reporting, was of great help during critical moments with her clear focus on technical questions and her supportive reassurance. The Austrian poet Christine Huber believed in this book and encouraged it since its inception in 1997. I'm endebted to Len Neufeld for his expert editorial input. A deep bow to all the people featured in the book, who graciously agreed to be videotaped by me: Daniela Beuren (20-21); Hil de Gard (63, 73); Gundl Herrnstadt (32-33, 43); Mara Herrnstadt (41); Christian Ide Hintze (36-37); Sara Hohenstein (20-21); Christine Huber (56-57, 67); Erwin Puls (36-37); Tania Puls (41); Shiran Shmerling (23, 26-27, 31, 47, 53, 64-65, 78, 88-89); Anika Szabó (25, 53, 58-59, 84-85); Tibor Tardos, Jr. (38-39); Esther van Messel (23, 31, 53); and Hilde Zimmermann (41, 45). I thank all of these friends and also, especially, Jackson Mac Low, who listened, looked, and helped every step of the way.

New York, 1999

UXUDO

For Berthe Tardos and for Jackson Mac Low

Alle Sünden aller Katzen zusammengefaßt

(Escalier) Strudlhof: the stairs that connect the high-lying
    eighth district of Vienna with the lower-lying
    ninth.
Also the subject of Heimito von Doderer's novel
Die Strudlhofstiege.

Wasquelham = an imaginary prinicipality featured in the
    novel *Rosa*, by Maurice Pons.

viszivilág = *[vee-see-vee-lahg]* = viszi = carries off / nimmt
    mit sich / emporte
                            (világ = world / Welt / monde)

Gefäß = container / vaisseau / tartály *[tar-tie]*

Mehrmalig = repeatedly
marvelous = merveilleux = csodálatos
Eigentum = possession / property
tiéd [tee-aid] = *yours / à toi / Dein*

Anglia = England = etc.

Eigentümlich = peculiar = strange = curious = odd =
    étrange = singulier = curieux = különös =
    sajátságos

completely. ganz und gar. (tout à fait)

All sins of all cats rolled into one.
Escalier Strudlhof bricolage.
Where do we come from and where do we
go?
Images, mon ami, ich smoke nicht mehr.
Gern would I do.

Sapristi

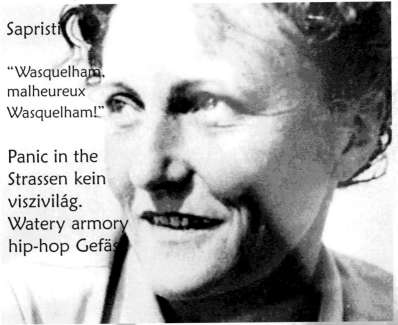

"Wasquelham,
malheureux
Wasquelham!"

Panic in the
Strassen kein
viszivilág.
Watery armory
hip-hop Gefä

Confidentially-timed refreshment options.
     Krakau.
Interrupt me donc, simplicity le chien.
Mehrmalig marvelous Eigentum, tiéd az Anglia.
Eigentümlich, tout à fait eigentümlich.

"So there they sat."

"You still have that letter?"
"They stayed like that for a long time."
"We already know."
 "At last some cool air came in."
 "Now they were all silent."

 "Come, sit down for a second."

"If only for five minutes."

"Da saßen sie also."

"Hast' den Brief noch?"
"Sie blieben lange so stehen."
"Wir wissen's bereits."
"Endlich kam die Kühle ins Zimmer."
"Nun schwiegen sie alle."

"Setz dich doch ein Augenblick her."

"Und sei es nur auf fünf Minuten."

Monkey ghost = majom szellem = fantôme singe

Direction couch = canapé de direction = irány-diván

Windfall sheets = unerwartete Glücksfallsblätter = draps d'aubaine

Sidérant = staggering, shattering
      Staggering = erstaunlich = Shattering = umwerfend
        Umwerfend = iszonyú, megrázó =
          sidérant *[see-day-rawnt]*

(Morticole = morticole = morticole = morticole = morticole = morticole)

quake = tremblement = Beben = rengés

Hopelessness amounts = quantités de désespoir = reménytelenségek

déselectionnez   le mois d'Avril

Affengespenst

For Barbara Barg

Affengespenst   Richtungsdivan.

Epidemic windfall sheets.

Inexplicable raw material.

Afterglow.

Sidérant morticole quake benefit.

Hoffnungslosigkeitsmengen.

Deselect.   Április.

23

Efnogla = *Efnogla* = **Efnogla** = Efnogla

Haut am Grass
  multiplicatering = multiplikatern

veinard [vey-nahr] Fr. *lucky one*

Durchschnittlich = average

Eigentlich = *in fact* = *en effet*

Ja chasch tänkke! [yah, hush tank-uh] Sw. Ger.: *yeah, right,*
or penses-tu. *(that's what* you *think.)*

Wir essen deine Ältern   *nous mangeons tes parents.*

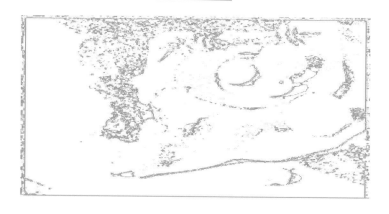

Efnogla - 1

Efnogla, skin on grass, multiplicatering delta veinard.
Durchschnittlich windy—je ne me le plastic wrap.
Eigentlich.
Ja chasch tänkke!
    Penses-tu.
        We eat your parents.

mondván *[mohnd-vahn]* = saying = sagend = disant

schreien [shrye-un] = to scream = hurler = üvölteni

szigorú *[see-gore-oo]* = stern, streng, sévère, dur, kemény

esténként *[ush-tayn-kaynt]* = evenings, abends, les soirs . . .

pistula = pistula = **pistula** = *pistula*

facets = Aspekte = facettes = szempontok

My soul, the wheel, my friend

Meine Seele, das Rad, mein Freund

Huldrych Zwingli, 1484-1531 (last entry in biographical section of Merriam Webster's Collegiate Dictionary, 10th ed.)

26

Efnogla -2

(We eat your parents)

somebody screams mondván schreien szigorú

esténként pistula eighty-nine facets.

Mon âme, das Rad, mon ami,

Zwingli came to a sweeter blank.

Glick = glick = glick = glcik = glick = glick = glick = glick

shano-glick = shano-glick = shano-glick = shano-glick

Elképzelhetetlen *[al-keyp-zal-hat-at-lan]* = unimaginable = unvorstellbar = inimaginable

Klebestoff *[klay-ber-shtohf]* = glue = colle = enyv

Ötvenen = fifty [of them] = une cinquantaine

to get on the bandwagon =
    csatlakozni diadalmaskodó mozgalomhoz =
        suivre le movement =
           sich dranhängen.

Efnogla - 3

(Sweeter blank)

Glick-glick armature en voiture shano-glick.

Elképzelhetetlen problems and sentiments

Arachnid juicy-fruit Klebestoff

Only the self can know

Ötvenen got on the bandwagon

Volga.

Hochgeduld [German. Pronounced: *HOEKH-gudoold*] = highpatience

Gekreuzung [G. pron: *gu-CROY-tsoong*] = becrossing

Jolie bête [French. pron: *ZHOW-ley bait*] pretty beast

Háromváros [Hungarian. pr: *HAH-rum-vah-rosh*]

Afterimage = Nachbild

Arcane bonkers = obskur spinnen

Unerträglich vielfach [G. pron. *OON-er-trayg-likh FEEL-fahck*] =
    manifold unbearable

Glupf! = glupf! = glupf!

Un oeil = one eye

Monkey ghosts (Affengespenste) after Barbara Barg.

Cucumber mosaic (n.1916): a virus disease esp. of cucumbers
that is transmitted chiefly by an aphid and produces mottled
foliage and often pale warty fruits.

Aalgrass.

Kuckuck.

Hochgeduld after nine from a fountain
Gekreuzung vielmehr, which is how it's done
Neighborly jolie bête
Give it time, háromváros.

Afterimage.

Bric-à-brac bitter fare arcane bonkers
Intriguing transitions and deepening sounds
Junk-dealer's abnormal squanderings Congo
Unerträglich vielfach living in truth.

Glupf!

Un oeil sees bluer and brighter than the other
Together they blend the perfect hue
Living with monkey ghosts, poverty variants,
Cucumber mosaics,
eelgrass & cuckoo.

Are you getting on this tram?

I don't know.

The final separation.
The farewell scene.
Then the street was empty.

She doesn't love him. And does he love her?
(But that's kid's stuff.)

The generous face.
And the warmth.
Slipping and sliding.

"Steigen Sie in den Tram?"
"Ich weiss nicht."

"Eine endgültige Trennung."
"Die Schluß-szene."
"Dann war die Gasse leer."

"Sie liebt ihn nicht. Und er sie?"
"(Aber das waren Kindereien.)"

"Das großzügige Gesicht."
"Und die Wärme."
"Eine Rutscherei."

"Did you maybe *want* to forget it?"

"I haven't noticed a thing."

"Except for the smell of the lavender."

"We barely spoke at all."

"I thought that was typical."

"Alright."

"Old fox."

"Enough."

Le mot d'une petite *plaisireuse*
    Schlüpfriges Geheimnis sensationellen Sexes.

Das Licht einer einzigen Galaxis.

Ein paar Lungen.

ArbeitsAmeisen

Word of a petite pleaser's
　　　　slippery secret of sensational sex.

The light of a single galaxy.

A pair of lungs.

A Seat, a Stretch, a Rivertwist

"The incidence of American women having triplets
has more than quadrupled in the last year."

Then you breathe: In with the odd, out with the odd.

Gargantuan figures

well above a googol.

Escargots

"la femelle des mouches choisit le male aux yeux attirants."

Snail filament
      par ici et par là *die Hände ermüden*

after you regard Sichtbarkeit
      und zu ahnen.

Alles ist Elend und Wucht

      wieder.

Egy, nulla, négy.

      two hundred and eighty times
      flown again.

"Female flies pick mates with sexy eyes."

Escargot filament
        hither and thither hands are tired
après-vous glance visibility
        and to have an inkling.
All miserere and blast.

                again.
One, zero, four.
        zweihundertachtzigmal
        wiedergeflogen.

hiába *[hee-ah-buw]* = to no avail = vergebens = inutilement

Ewigkeitstätigkeit = occupation-eternity

Ráncostánc = *[ron-tsosh-tahnts]* = wrinkly dance =
     Knittertanz = danse-ridée

griffonade = griffonade = griffonade = griffonade
(griffonage = scribbling [Gekritzel])
(griffon = a kind of dog, or a griffin, the mythological
half eagle half lion.)

rictus = Sperrweite
     kiván = *[key-vahn]* = wishes / wünscht / désire

Räuberträume *[roy-bur-troy-mu]* = robber-dreams
     = rêves-voleur

follitude = follitude = follitude = follitude = follitude

uxudo = uxudo = uxudo = uxudo = uxudo = uxudo

Lorraine hug-a-bee hiába
Wanderwunderbare Ewigkeitstätigkeit
Ráncostánc.
Objet sécurisé de griffonade.
Daedalus pagination
        rictus kiván.

Ivan was terrible.

Who am I really?

Räuberträume
follitude.

Uxudo.

(Magyarul: hunyú)

Wer konnte wissen? Wie das alles enden würde?

Das Menschenhirn ist eine faule Angelegenheit.
Sie war eine frühe Denkerin.

Sie hinterließ den Flughafen und ihre Kastagnetten.

Die Sprache der Schimpansen wurde erst später erwähnt.

Left the airport and her castanets behind.

The language of chimpanzees
    came into question later.

Who knew?

Who knew how things would turn out?
The human brain was a lazy affair.
She was an early thinker.

Left the airport and her castanets behind.

The language of chimpanzees
      came into question later.

Love

Il y'a longtemps que je t'aime,
Jamais je ne t'oublierai.

Il y a longtemps que je t'aime, jamais je ne t'oublierai.

Bild

Gelbe Kurve von links nach rechts.
Schön sanft. Ja. Kann warten.

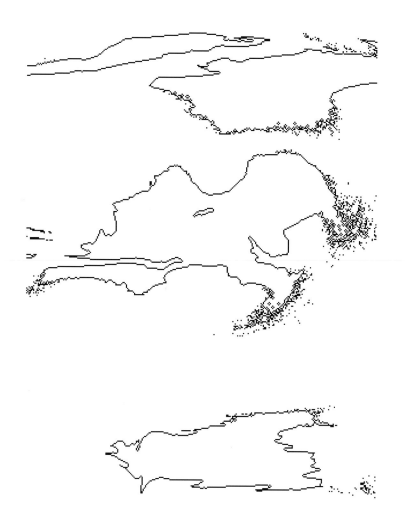

PAINTING

Yellow curve from left to right.
Nice and soft—Yes—Waiting.

Sommetrommel

vom Hörensagen greifbare Gelassenheit

Szép anyag *(sayp A-nyawg)* = beautiful material, schönes Stoff

Akkor tüszkölni = *UK-core   toos-kulney* = to then sneeze
(niessen)

Blimpinault defunction = blimpinault defunction

Édes érzékenykedés = sweet touchiness
Aydush Air-zay-kunykudaysh.

süße Empfindlichkeit

Szép anyag didn't run Summerdrum

Hearsay tactile serenity, Zelda.

What you see, is.

Akkor tüszkölni shelter.

Blimpinault defunction.

Form of happiness—érzékenykedés.

This is how the
brain works: et
patati et patata . . .

That petite
animal down
there at your feet.

She Put It Mildly

Tired out by long winter nights,
she took the daylight, with its first sip of tea
tasting like nectar, as a gift.

Ragaszkodó madness.
(raw-gaw-skoe-doe = attached, ~ing)

She put it so mildly she couldn't be heard by
those who were used to the din.

She explored processes and suffered.

Vomit and badgerings, cruelty bleedings of
merdivorous* bannister fracas.

*Gänsehäufel*** bathing beauty.

*dung-eating
** a beach near Vienna [lit. trans: geese piles]

So there they sat.

Tombé [*fallen* / gefallen]

Gewurzeltidé =Gewurzeltidé = Gewurzeltidé

Eigenschaft = quality *[eye-gun-shuft]*

Graben: a square in Vienna.

Toowomba 1

Da saßen sie also.

Tombé, tombé, gewurzeltidé.

Tombé gewurzeltidé Eigenschaft am Graben.

Körülnézek *[**ker**-ruel-nay-zack]* [körül-nehsek]
= ich schaue mich um = I look around me = je regarde
autour de moi *[cœurule-nézeque]*.

    Ceux qui ont de l'eau le boivent.

Gürtelschnallen, Zigarren, *nervousness.*

Toowomba 2

Körülnézek.

People who have water drink it.

Beltbuckles, cigars, die Nervosität.

At last.
The frame of the thought = der Rahmen der Idee
einrahmen, ablegen, kategorisierende Gedanken.

allerschwab = *allerschwab* = **allerschwab** = allerschwab
miamander = *miamander* = *miamander* = *miamander*
touffenade = touffenade = touffenade = touffenade
gelinkami = gelinkami = *gelinkami* = gelinkami
pensura = pensura = pensura = pensura = pensura

Toowomba 3

Na endlich.

Le cadre de l'idée: framing, filing, categorizing thought.

Allerschwab miamander touffenade gelinkami pensura.

Newspaper.

Toowomba 4

Diligenti levelentent benevolency ahm sirkan
bela viadji hovala.
Ieta tanbimin.   Zeitung.

Geschwollen
Gonflé
Bedagadt

eine süße kleine Nagelhaut

(une petite épiderme mignonne)

Toowomba 5

Swollen, I don't know.
Cute little cuticle from Utica.
Krakatoa vérité.

Lautstärke

Vociferousness and disinfection.

Odorifera millensis.

Odiens los angelensis.

Odiferous = odiferous = odiferous = odiferous

Situationen erlebt und erinnert

Mitgefühl [mitt-gu-fuel] = compassion

Ebsilgator = ebsilgator = ebsilgator = ebsilgator

cip szám ~ cipõ szám *[shoe size]* {TSIper sahm}
cip szám ~ cipõ szám *[Schuh Größe]* [*Zipö sam*]

Toowomba 7

Odiferous situations experienced and recalled
Wanntenferra Mitgefühl
Ebsilgator cip szám.

Unique promise-foam
    [ayn-tsig-ahr-tigger far-**shpreck**ungs-shawm]

Blensk = Blensk = Blensk = Blensk = Blensk = Blensk
Viriusmogen = viriusmogen = viriusmogen
Bliskily = bliskily = bliskily = bliskily = bliskily = bliskily

vanity = vanité = Eitelkeit = hiábavalóság *[hee-ah-buh-vu-low-shahg]* [hi-a-ba-valoschaag]

magidé = magidé = magidé = magidé = magidé = magidé

Einzigartiger Versprechungsschaum.

Blensk Viriusmogen.

Bliskily vanity magidé.

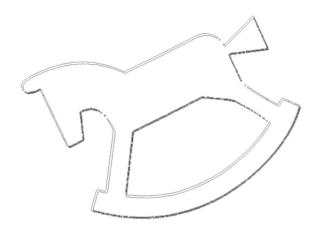

Essayons ça—1

Poésie de pouvoir = Machtdichtung

Was macht lächerlich?
Ablehnung macht lächerlich.

Pressé contre la jambe du poète, le chat s'endort.

Est-ce préférable de ne pas agir du tout que d'avoir tort?

Jobb nem cselekedni mint rosszul tenni?

Ich frage nur.

Eine vorschnelle Antwort führte den Impulsiven irre.

L'impulsive s'est égaré à cause de sa réponse hâtive.

Let's Try This - 1

Good, good, good, many worlds, good.
Power poetry.

What it is that makes ridiculous?
Rejection makes ridiculous. (Rejection makes
ridiculous.)

Pressed against the poet's leg, the cat sleeps
soundly.

Is it better not to act at all than to act wrong?
Better not to be than to be off?
I'm just asking.

A hasty reply led the impulsive one astray.

Essayons ça—2

kavicsok [kaw-vee-choke] [ka-vitschok] =
pebbles = cailloux

---

látvány [laht-vahny] *[lat-vany]* = spectacle

kalandor [kaw-lawn-door] *[ka-lan-dor]* =
adventurer

Zugzwang: *in chess: to be forced to move / to be in a spot*

[die Kunst widerspiegelt nicht das Leben
sondern den Betrachter.]

Albright: Portrait painter from Chicago [known for
his painting in the Hollywood movie *The Picture of
Dorian Gray.* ["All art is at once surface and sym-
bol. Those who go beneath the surface do so at
their own peril."]

gewirkelt = gewirkelt = gewirkelt = gewirkelt

Let's Try This —2

Pebble-territory kavicsok plus ou moins
Brooklyn-bound látvány kalandor makes you
think.

The emperor's clothes are made of the best
material.

Aberrating roar cassette.

Easy bookpacks, stars, jealousness.

A long flat narrow stick used to stir with.

There is no rush here, no zugzwang.

The audience's willingness to be amused is not
to be taken lightly.

It is the spectator, and not life, that art really
mirrors. (Ivan Le Lorraine Albright)

Buchstaben gewirkelt.

crafty = wily = 𝔰𝔠𝔥𝔩𝔞𝔲 = 𝔯𝔞𝔣𝔣𝔦𝔫𝔦𝔢𝔯𝔱

[foor-fan-gosh] *[fuhr-fahngosch]*
[lawn-gosh] *[lahn-gosch]*

edge-reah shew-**ye**ddur
𝔇𝔢𝔦𝔫 𝔚𝔢𝔰𝔢𝔫 𝔨𝔞𝔫𝔫𝔰𝔱 𝔡𝔲 𝔫𝔦𝔠𝔥𝔱 ä𝔫𝔡𝔢𝔯𝔫

falling deeper

and deeper

𝔐𝔞𝔫𝔠𝔥𝔢 𝔖𝔲𝔪𝔪𝔢.
The fly, the feather, catishness.
nam ross =
not bad

Furfangos - 1

Furfangos lángos
Egyre lejjebb süllyedő
Deeply fallen

Brèque mizimungard
Apriness brahma
Seveben spiralaire
Doctrin em shopronique
Viza shnengen absalee.

Iyeh, Iyeh, Ilyander!

Szivebelle, you can't change your essence.
Some sum, some sum.
Die Fliege, die Feder, die Katzenhaftigkeit.
Nem rossz *sinegard zumm,* oh!

Verstärke den Regen
[ron-dah] ugly = hässlich

Langeweile Nachlass Verwüstung.
                            Socken.

Der Regen.

Wayne = ein Name
wrap = Umhang

Gleichgültiger Verrat noch wer kümmert sich nicht?

Reinforce the rain, ronda Rhonda

Affectionnado simpabulba

Timpa na gulna

Sinfa da dolba

Tchicke-bam tchicke-boom

Efligtelli shvah-rahm

Boredom residue havoc.
Amok stanaïc sock.

The rain.

Iflegeldy sundershaw.

Vastly bushvid apsalhatten
Evingot.

Varna mishnol semirack.

Settledon *wayne wrap*

Indifferent betrayal nor who doesn't care?

Dante Gabriel Rossetti, painter and poet, 1828–1882.

Pre-Raphaelite Brotherhood

(John Everett Millais
(William Holman Hunt
(John Ruskin

Thoughts towards Nature in Poetry, Literature, and Art

Elizabeth Siddal ("Lizzie")
(and Fanny Cornforth and Jane Burden)

Christina Georgina Rossetti, poet, 1830–1894
Goblin Market:

One had a cat's face
One whisked a tail
One tramped at a rat's pace
One crawled like a snail
One like a wombat prowled obtuse and furry
One like a ratel tumbled hurry scurry

For DGR and the PRB

A range of talents can bring hostile criticism.

Mother Frances Polidori, granddaughter of
Byron's doctor and companion in exile.
A crucial moment.
            Millais, Hunt, and later Ruskin.

The Girlhood of Mary the Virgin,
                Venus Verticordia.
A deep belief in the unbelievable.

                water
            Watershed
                water

Lizzie was everywhere.
After she oh-deed on laudanum,
        He turned in his oil brush for watercolor.

        Christina is . . .
            "Sleeping at Last"

[Fudd-razz] *[fodd-rahs]*
hairdresser / *Friseur*

Antimaterie

*flirtation [lee-buh-**ley**]*

Regierungshemdhose

Aufträger ['æplikeite']

Kanone ['krækedzæk]

apricot = Aprikose ['eiprikot]

Fodrász pink apricot
Antimatter Liebelei
government union suit
Feline indifference
Applicator Crackerjack

Antimatter union suit   Fodrász pink

Crackerjack Liebelei
Fodrász pink government
Feline indifference
Antimatter union suit

CON-LON— 1

Awouls, awools, those guys! tooth-tooth!
Anger— cough— detest— pardon— NO!

In the middle of a murmur— sit.

Friction macht nichts.

Transition strings Nan-
Carrow
        Ketten játszanak (two are playing)
(es spielen zwei)

Schön, daß man mich schreiben läßt.
(szép, hogy hagynak írni)

Atmen back in Jazz
[to breathe] *[ahtmun]*

I Fagott *[German: pron. "forgot" = bassoon]*
my bassoon zenészek.
        [ZUH-nay-sack] = musicians

Vibrancy the page turner.
Prestissimo.

Are cuffs in again? *[sind aufgeschlagene*
Hosen wieder modern?]

Lábbal kapaszkodik. Lábaival.
[lah-bawl kaw-paw-skoa-dik] = hangs on by his / her feet.
[lah-baw-ee-vawl] = with his / her feet.

Echte Americana via saxophone and bassoon.
Van *[vawn]* = *(there is)* exuberance spannend
[**shpahn**-end] = exciting

Gershwinesque Hindemithy

Tatta-rattá   tatta-rattá

nem egy akaratos (nicht penetrant)
[nam edge aw-kaw-raw-tosh] not pushy

Vagány *[vaw-gahny]* *[untranslatable, akin to "daring."]*

amused seriousness *amid* serious amusement
Good jumpy *versus* bad jumpy

Depraved conditions.
That bastard!

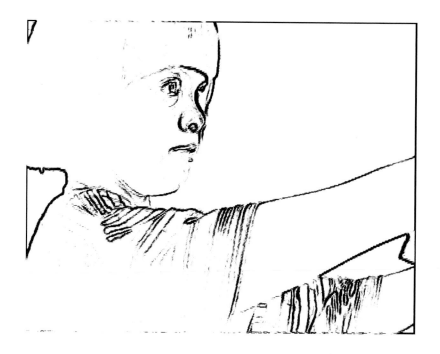

Looking forward into the garden
behind her

she finds

zee bleaked in dane garden
hint-err zick
oond fiend-at

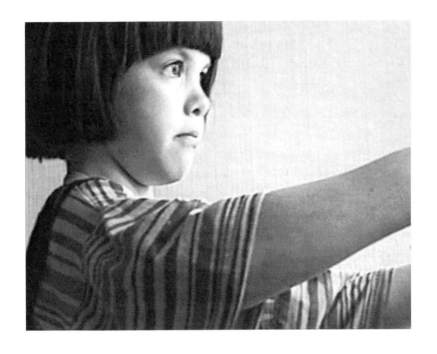

Sie blickt in den Garten hinter
sich

und findet

luking forwart intu
ze garden biheind hör
schie feinds

Dee *Eye*-luh

Die Eile zunächst
    a growing independence
        so what will she do?
            Elle danse la fumée, so
              ich bin nicht ich.
You believe in flexibility and you're in business.
    Speak about the waves. *Parlez moi des vagues.*
    Not vague waves, distinct ones.

    Qui lira ça, rira.
        (Key leera sah, reerah.)

Nem kell mindig veszekedni, children. *Jólmegmondom.* (one word)

Nam *quelle* meen-dig veh-seh-kehd-knee. Yoale-meg-
moan-dome. (egy szó).

Sh~ sh~~ sh~~~

UXUDO was printed in an edition of 1,000
as a joint project of Tuumba Press and O Books

The acid-free and 100% recycled paper is
70 pound Fortune Matte, 500 ppi Text Stock

Printed by Thomson-Shore, Inc. Dexter, Michigan

Designed and typeset by Anne Tardos

The book was composed using the programs
Fractal Design Painter, Adobe® Photoshop®, Adobe® PageMaker®, and
Microsoft® Word. Video images were digitized using the video capture tool
Microsoft VidCap.

The font most used throughout this book was Garamond.
Several other TrueType fonts were also used.

Other books by Anne Tardos

Cat Licked the Garlic, Vancouver, B.C.: Tsunami Editions, 1992
Mayg-shem Fish, Elmwood, Connecticut: Potes & Poets, 1995

Other works listed on http://members.xoom.com/Tardos